CW01391613

The Shouting Tories

The Bread and Roses Poetry Award Anthology 2022

**Edited by
Mike Quille**

**Introduced by
Alan Morrison**

No amount of cajolery, and no attempts at ethical or social seduction, can eradicate from my heart a deep burning hatred for the Tory Party. So far as I am concerned they are lower than vermin.

—Aneurin Bevan

CULTURE MATTERS

First published 2022 by Culture Matters.
Culture Matters Co-Operative Ltd. promotes a socialist and progressive
approach to art, culture and politics. See www.culturematters.org.uk

Contents

Verse of adversity

By Alan Morrison, Associate Editor, Culture Matters

It's a privilege to introduce this the sixth Culture Matters Bread & Roses Poetry Award anthology comprising politically apposite, polemical poems by 24 shortlisted poets and the five winning entrants, Nick Allen, Jennifer Johnson, Tracey Pearson, Steve Taylor and David Williams.

This is poetry of witness to the extraordinary vicissitudes of recent times: the long lingering twilight of the pandemic, the cataclysmic war in Ukraine, the belated defenestration of Boris Johnson, the contagion of national grief following the death of Elizabeth Windsor (during which any public expressions of republicanism were effectively verboten), the energy crisis and 'warm hubs' being provided in public libraries for those who can't afford to heat their homes properly this winter.

But the backcloth to this anthology's publication is equally tumultuous: the recent financial crisis triggered by the morally bankrupt and fiscally counterintuitive Truss-Kwarteng mini-budget; Truss's subsequent defenestration as prime minister (after just 44 days, the shortest premiership in British history by some margin, the previous record having been George Canning who died in office after 119 days); the prospect of spending cuts and a second age of austerity; and yet another unelected Tory prime minister foisted on a nation screaming out for a general election which would almost certainly lead to a Labour landslide and a Tory wipe out, judging by the polls.

This is a particularly frustrating place for us to be, and a deeply perilous one, since it is symptomatic of a crisis of democracy. It feels as if the British electorate has been defenestrated from its suffrage, as a power-corrupted Tory party treats our democracy as its own private fiefdom, foisting prime minister after prime minister on us. Two of them were chosen by a tiny and unrepresentative blue rinse membership, culmination of the antediluvian processes of the publicly unaccountable 1922 Committee. The third prime minister (in so many months), Rishi Sunak, was effectively coronated by the 1922 Committee's Chair and kingmaker, 'Sir' Graham Brady—a second accession in two months, after that of Charles Windsor.

There has been, then, plenty to protest about, as ever. To protest effectively in poetry requires elements of tonal control, prosodic craftsmanship, and dexterity at rhetorical devices. The poems in this anthology—to use litotes —do not disappoint in these respects. The poetical approaches from the 29 poets are many and various, but broadly range from poetry of witness to poetry of testament.

Ruth Aylett's 'Obituary' is a beautifully composed witness to what seems to be the death of a refugee forced to beg on the streets of London. Its Larkinesque eloquence is imbued with a palpable empathy:

> Crowds flocked to the tube; he lurched the other way
> longing for empty space, uninhabited blocks,
> freedom from the buses and the car exhausts,
> the homeless in the doorways with their dogs...
>
> Staggering and chilled, face damp with aimless rain
> or maybe also tears, he felt something like a pain,
> a tightening band inside his stomach or perhaps his chest
> that drove him through the unfamiliar streets
> until at last he wandered to the Thames edge
> with lights across it that he knew he could not reach.
> Canary Wharf point blocks towered in high contempt,
> the river's black water leered; abandoned by his past
> he wobbled helplessly, dropped his box
> and fell, his brain ringing with the sound of brass.

Tracey Pearson's wonderfully titled 'Somewhere a Tory Flaps its Wings' is another empathetic poem of witness which takes a broader brush approach to the state of society:

> a foodbank volunteer   pretends not to know
> her neighbour   adds an extra packet of biscuits
>
> a child eats cereal for breakfast   dinner
> and tea   now poverty's on the menu
>
> a veteran sleeps in a tent   under a bridge
> waits for the day   the bombs stop
>
> a mental health support worker   pops
> an antidepressant   prays for a quiet day

Emma Purshouse's 'Unsuitable Places—the YTS girl from the Old Vic Hotel remembers' seems to be painting a harrowing picture of the contemporary plight of refugee asylum seekers in Britain's 'hostile environment':

> Kid's faces pixilate in cracked frames. Hung out to dry
> washing is bunting in first floor windows. A red jumper reaches
> out its arms. Floral trousers press themselves to the glass.

And there are many poems of personal testament to our times. Mark Cassidy's '(Fear of the) Unfinished' is a powerful expression of a poet's sense of powerlessness in the face of political oppression, and yet in its own quiet way is hopeful:

> What, in the ever-perishing now,
> is measure of each day?
> Silent poems do not show
> the little difference protest brings.
> Nor the permanence of revolution.

Equally moving is Keith Hill's self-flagellating 'Democratic Deficit':

> I hate the man that I've become,
> abdicating responsibility,
> carping, complaining.
> I know what I need to do.
> Get involved, solicit, supplant.

While Steve Taylor's wry 'The Red Wall' ploughs a similar furrow but from a more ironic viewpoint:

> I have inherited the laziness of my Class I'm afraid.
>
> Punish me.

Steve Pottinger's '(don't) read all about it!' courts adage with its apposite closing couplet:

> ... Don't buy the lies they sell.
> The stories that we need to hear are the ones that they don't tell.

Liam O'Neill's 'Mr Cameron's Foodbank (Or, When tone-deaf privilege fails to read the room)' comments on the moral hypocrisy of the former prime minister having the brass neck to do a photo call 'helping out' at one of the foodbanks necessitated by his government's dismantling of the welfare safety net.

Moira Garland's curious 'Wash Your Mouth Out' presents the disappearance of certain words, or the actions and feelings associated with those words, all of which relate to defiance, as a metaphor for incremental political disempowerment—the banned words presented in a fading grey text:

> ... Our *fists* did not provide
>
> *resistance.* By day seven *questioning* had gone,
> then day eight lost *incandescence.*
> Each day words are cleansed,
> our language trafficked,
>
> shipped out to become
> frothing, bubbly, empty, soap.

Jennifer Johnson's 'Uprising' has a revolutionary defiance:

> One day, each stone will rise
> the second we feel their tread.
> Make sure we trip up the lot,
> watch them plunge to join us.

Jenny Mitchell's 'Levelling Up' is written from the viewpoint of the daughter of a Downing Street cleaner during national lockdown when Boris Johnson played host to a continuous wine-soaked 'lock in':

> Our PM starts a waddling dance, nods their head,
> wine spilling from the glass to toast the bacchanal
> as they sing out of tune The Winner Takes It All ten
> times, louder-still as Abba fades into the fetid air.
> Mother tries to crawl away but cat-calls are renewed
> for her to polish shoes, kneeling on the carpet.

There are also historical reflections on the perennial class and wealth divides of British society, as in Ciarán O'Rourke's 'Concerning the Conditions of the Working Poor' subtitled 'After Friedrich Engels, 1820-1895':

> the stony huts of peasants, rotting in the rain,
> famine shaking like a palsy
> across the stunted hills. Beyond
> these shrunken villages, long avenues of loss,
> a splendid greenery survives—on lawns
> the leisured landlords keep in fine repair.

And Joe Williams' satirical 'Jacob Marley's Ghost Returns to London':

> I believed all the rich men
> would fall, Ebenezer,
> but no—they have more now
> than we could have imagined.
> I should not have undervalued
> the resilience of greed,
> the resolve of men with power
> to absolve themselves of guilt,
> transfer the stench of blame to the oppressed.
>
> What say you, Ebenezer—
> will you join me tonight?
> There is a great deal of work to be done.

While Antony Owen's 'Our Street of Ghosts' is a beautifully constructed reminiscence of Eighties industrial decline which has some striking aphorismic flourishes:

> I remember when Thatcher killed all our fathers
> we gazed at snow making alps of factory rooftops
> an orange Cortina billowed in the distance
> ...
> smoking inside his ark afloat on a tulip sea
> building his ovum of old Cortina parts.
> ...
> My Father's hair now resembles that snowy factory roof
> it covers the stained-glass of his derelict eyes.

Owen brilliantly encapsulates political comment in heightened poetic images—a perfect example of a type of proletarian poetry which William

Empson once described as 'Covert Pastoral':

> Last night he vacced my fake grass free of real leaves
> a bee pulsed on the wilting lavender
> it had lost the will to return to its hive
> the death of summer is odourless.

Finally, I'm honoured to have had a poem included alongside such powerful companions, and even more so that its title has been chosen for this anthology as a whole. Undoubtedly the boisterously (public-) schoolboyish and obnoxious aural spectacle of green benches of Tory MPs roaring *"MORE!—MORE!"* when they like one of their prime minister's swipes at the despatch box is one of the most grating and dispiriting of sounds. It is a firm reminder why the antiquated, juvenile, adversarial architecture of Parliament is so direly in need of reform and modernisation. I chose the form of a villanelle for its refrains in order to convey this sense of ear-pummelling repetition.

So there's plenty for us to be shouting about after twelve years of Tory rule and the prospect of austerity 2.0. Our nation is screaming out for change like never before, and we know this will never come in any substantial or progressive sense under a Tory government. Though bowdlerised of its Corbyn-era socialist authenticity by the overly cautious centrist Keir Starmer, a Labour Government would still be infinitely more preferable to the Tories, and we can only hope that a general election comes sooner than later and—as the polls copiously signpost—wipes the blue Yahoos off the political map.

In many ways the space of real political Opposition at the moment is being occupied by the trade unions, the CWU, PCS and RMT in particular. The RMT's Mick Lynch and Eddie Dempsey, two astonishingly articulate and powerful speakers, are an inspiration for us all at this time. Enough is indeed Enough.

In the meantime, we continue to resist, in our protests and in our poetries, in our protesting poetries, and anthologies such as these that are at the vanguard of this verse of adversity.

Nick Allen

after the conference

brothers and sisters of the October night   poets of this endless northern rainfall when it is wet underfoot and millions of light years are gathered in each kerbside puddle   what charts should we use to navigate our way as we pass under hallelujah cranes saluting the withheld universe between neon-fronted stores and cyclops taxi-cabs cruising to take us to unthought of destinations   and we do this to ourselves   we drink our red wine and we listen to the finest poet the land has to offer as she shakes out her words of light and water and dreaming and gods and time and we swim and we swim   to keep our heads above euphoria   and we are the only ones out here apart from the homeless guys in the shop doorway   the bench sleepers   the guys who raise tents in underpasses and out on the sparse grasses of parks where they lie and dream of sleep to wrap them against this wind that knifes down Deansgate   cleaving the sadness of our shame in autumn while they wait on inevitable winter   and we all know that days ago the architects of this misery were toasting their brilliance their once again entitled seat at the head of table   the disdain is tangible their stench lingers over the gutters and drains and the overflowing bins of sodden Manchester   they have earned this they reassure each other and you have not - the thoughts unspoken twin   and the lonesome poets of the Lancastrian night push noses against another plate glass window sighing all their disenfranchised heartbreak   and my hair is pressed to my skull like a migraine or a bad dream

a young man walks by   the cuckoo mouth of his unzipped backpack yawns to the sky because he is gathering rain against the forecast shortages of everything   my train rolls above these ghost-lit offices empty now of the last worker trying to impress with their deranged durability and lack of imagination and all the waited-for-lives that wait as shadows behind projection screen curtains of student blocks   all the new not-real money that floods between fingers of the not-at-all well-to-do who gamble this debt against a possible future   and where will we find ourselves brothers and sisters where will we find ourselves now that we live in a land that can only dream backwards   where prospects are things that only old money can buy   where will we find ourselves with our soft boots wet to the skin of our aching blisters and heels that rub and toes that rub and the soaking hems of our trousers that we just cant keep out of the rising waters   and the wind picks up litter in Albert Square where there is no xmas tree and there is no fair and any poet that there was is long gone and tucked softly in his dreams   and now coffee-slow and footsore slogging through a short night of well-bottom sleep   I crawl into the next available morning my mind back in the carriage with homeless Douglas who hasnt got a ticket and worries that he is out past the hostel curfew and slow sly steals my bag of nuts and asks me again if I have a cigarette or at least a Rizla and I repeat that I dont smoke and he worries again about the curfew   and would we even recognise truth if she walked by in her threadbare coat

WE WANT BREAD, AND ROSES TOO!

Ruth Aylett

Obituary

"Drunk and alone among the indifferent lights
In stark unending streets of granite and glass
He ducked his head to avoid illusory stalactites
And fell .his brain ringing with the sound of brass"
—Louis MacNeice

Janet of HR failed to meet his eyes and said
the news though bad could not be unexpected:
go right now and there will be a settlement.
But what to tell his friends, and his former colleagues?
The after-work pub in its afternoon lull
had that false smile of welcome, and there
he emptied his wallet then waved his plastic card
until the brusque barman told him to depart;
clutched to his chest the box of his whole working life,
drunk and alone among the indifferent lights.

For twenty years that office was his everything
constant when he moved from flat to house
and back to flat, through marriage, child, divorce.
Fighting the slowing brain and thickening waist
in a weekly five-a-side with his office mates.
The old company gave up, they got a new boss
from private equity owners who squeezed the assets
which he was not one of, just another cost.
As night ate the horizon he was lost
in stark unending streets of granite and glass.

Crowds flocked to the tube; he lurched the other way
longing for empty space, uninhabited blocks,
freedom from the buses and the car exhausts,
the homeless in the doorways with their dogs,
that maybe he'd be joining very soon.
London's oranged clouds moved in sudden winds,
a story read in school drifted in his mind:
that life was just a cave with shadows on its sides
all our day-to-day created by uneven flickering lights.
He ducked his head to avoid illusory stalactites.

Staggering and chilled, face damp with aimless rain
or maybe also tears, he felt something like a pain,
a tightening band inside his stomach or perhaps his chest
that drove him through the unfamiliar streets
until at last he wandered to the Thames edge
with lights across it that he knew he could not reach.
Canary Wharf point blocks towered in high contempt,
the river's black water leered; abandoned by his past
he wobbled helplessly, dropped his box
and fell, his brain ringing with the sound of brass.

Holly Bars

Arsehole

I drive past Tapi Carpets and remember the woman in the pub, going on about being promoted to manager there; she was actually called Karen. I felt sorry for her; she talked about carpets all night. I feel sorry for everyone nowadays, the way they can't shut the fuck up about the government, as if it even exists, and it is not just people in a room who didn't get enough hugs, having their expenses paid for. This is a shallow view but I am a tired woman who has never drunk the Kool Aid. I don't even know what the fuck Kool Aid is. I had my respect for institutional constructs smashed when my paeedo got away with it. And since then I have been skimming my flat body along the top of the pool, like the water's surface is soft glass. Karen is well in it, half-way down the tank, with her important badge and her Bluetooth headset, or whatever. All her staff parties and Christmas fairy lights. And her shitting joy.

Bob Beagrie

The Gresham Angels

Beyond the door, they say, is one
of the roughest parts of a town
the country's written off, an off-hand
joke on quiz shows, a place
of ethnic tensions, anti-social behaviour,
poverty, crime, aggressive addictions;
like tonight, hopping into a taxi to head
into town, the cab will be blocked by a car
stopped bang in the middle of the road
as a woman in her sixties, drunk as a skunk,
hurls herself at it, yanking the handles,
hammering fists against the windows and
calling everyone inside worse than shite,
who'll then pile out and knock her to the floor
while neighbours pour from their front doors
to join the fray under the face of a full moon
peering from behind chimneypots, but that's
tonight and this is the morning when the
Gresham Angels float down terraced streets
between Laycock Park, Tan-Tastic, Tesco
Express, Y.K.Chow's, and the gym,
full to the brim with bubbles, grins, giggles,
Besties Forever, their bleached hair
in matching ponytails, eyelids heavy
with false lashes fluttering like oil-clogged
moth wings, to deliver lost car keys
back to distraught owners, who've spent
yesterday scouring the house retracing
footsteps, rechecking the sideboard
for the umpteenth time, down the back

of the sofa, under the sofa, coat pockets,
trouser pockets, fridge, bins, bedside cabinet,
under the bed, random drawers, computer desk,
to give up and sit skulking, eyes panning
the surfaces like searchlights and whispering
'Where the fuck...!' until the surprise knock
this morning and those Gresham Angels
smiling at the sheer joy of helping, and asking
'Have you lost your car keys? We found them
down the street, we've tried all the cars
and they open this one here.' They point
to my car and hand them over, then drift
around the corner with a wave like a carefree
Spring breeze leaving you weighing up
the good, the bad and the beautiful.

Breid an Roses

Mark Cassidy

(Fear of the) Unfinished

Last night's glasses, this morning's mugs
are unwashed, strewn about.
Up to one's armpits in unbrushed hair
and grubbled bedsheets, cleaning starts
with teeth and hands.

Ironing unfolds on the unswept floor.
Cupboard doors that will not fasten
remain unfixed.
Frayed attachments wait
on calls to friends not made.

Step outside. Pruning, overdue.
Fences to whitewash and patch up.
The news is closing in.
Beyond an uncut lawn, the earth
demands to be undug.

What, in the ever-perishing now,
is measure of each day?
Silent poems do not show
the little difference protest brings.
Nor the permanence of revolution.

Julie Easley

Resist

when everything they do is designed to break
you, revel in the truth you hurt them by being alive
your existence alone is an act of rebellion

make noise
make noise with others
release your battle cry
repeat

create your community
take comfort in knowing community is a power
they will never understand, for when poverty
is snapping
at your heels they will try to other you
they will other your neighbours
they will other everyone around you but themselves
resist
embrace the things that connect and learn from your differences

when you are cold know they use your taxes
to warm their lovers' beds
when you are hungry know they use your taxes
to feed their lobbying bellies
when you are drowning know they use your taxes
to keep themselves afloat
remember

spell out the cruelty of their conservatism
spell out the cruelty of their classism
spell out the cruelty of their cronyism

spell out their cruelty
speak up for the sanctioned
speak up for the vulnerable
speak up for the immigrant for one day that may be you
speak up for yourself because they want you to be silent

make noise
make noise with others
release your battle cry
repeat

BARA A CHAWS!

Moira Garland

Wash your mouth out

To start with we took it as generosity
cutting through extraneous vocabulary.
Emails were not allowed *kind*
in any sense: *type* or *considerate*.

Next, *friend* went, round the phoney bend.
They sent out an ultimatum: no place
for *comrades*. On day four we could not
disagree. Our *fists* did not provide

resistance. By day seven *questioning* had gone,
then day eight lost *incandescence*.
Each day words are cleansed
our language trafficked,

shipped out to become
frothing, bubbly, empty, soap.

Oz Hardwick

Ceasefire

It's late afternoon, though the Sun still hasn't risen, and the weather's still drawing lots to decide who'll be first over the top. We're in the No Man's Land of the year, with all its distrust and temporary truces, its rigid smiles at the negotiating table, its conciliation and concealed weapons; and here I am, trench deep in uncertainty, my bullet holed white flag unfit for any outcome. I tell myself it's only weather, it's only light; but every official metaphor—from the war on terror to levelling up—has left me unsatisfied with anything but death or glory. The day's darkness catches up with creeping night, the only light the tip of my unfiltered tab. Storms approach in camouflage, belly down in the trampled garden, and all the days 'til Christmas are gathering in the War Room. By the time the Sun rises, it's raining call-up papers and telegrams from the Palace, my crystal set memory reminds me it's a long, long way to Tipperary, and a scab-kneed newsboy promises peace in our time if we don't nuke the fuckers first.

Martin Hayes

what resistance means

it first bores itself into you when you are younger
the type of music you listen to
that catches you on your own
18 and naked inside your bedroom
air-guitaring in front of the mirror

next
some catastrophic event
will shatter you

then as you get a bit older
you will compartmentalise that
then the loneliness will kick in
and you will sleep under the wild moon
dreaming ugly dreams

then when you get your first job
it will be there
crystallising inside your fingertips
tapping away at their buttons
trying to make it all feel okay
trying to make it all seem fine
then when you take those fingertips home with you
it will hurt

if it doesn't hurt then you haven't got it
and you will never know what it means

later
your voice will become hoarse from constantly trying to speak for it

your heart will become scarred and miss the occasional pump
from constantly trying to fight for it
your lungs will become black and your liver bloated
from the nights when you smoked and drunk to it

then even later
when you are on your own in the dark wood of sleep
you will meet it
and you will nod to it
and if it passes you by without nodding back
you will know that its appearance
at least meant that you came close
but that your soul wasn't strong enough
this time to change anything
but that next time it could

Keith Hill

Democratic Deficit

I hate the man that I've become,
a man who spoils his ballot paper by drawing a penis,
a flaccid penis, veined and wrinkled.
Impotent,
like our democracy.

Dodgy dossier, devious drinks,
expenses exploitation, Brexit blundering.
Enough is enough.
Enough of the shameless self-serving,
the Eton elite, the Eton mess.
The rich get richer, the poor get food banks.
A national shame, politicians to blame.

I hate the man that I've become,
abdicating responsibility,
carping, complaining.
I know what I need to do.
Get involved, solicit, supplant.

Jennifer Johnson

Uprising

We're fed up of being walked over,
always taken for granted,
only for them to protect
their precious shoes from the mud.

What with the Council cuts
we've been badly neglected.
Most of us are cracking up,
going to pieces under the strain.

Let us raise some corners,
send a few flying head-first,
laugh at the bruised faces
of those who never look at us.

One day, each stone will rise
the second we feel their tread.
Make sure we trip up the lot,
watch them plunge to join us.

John F. Keane

Hey You There!

Hey you there, count your blessings
because you could be a fish living
in the dark twilight zone of the sea
with no IQ and a light on your head
knowing jack shit about anything
not even sunlight, let alone apps or
mobile phones or the Premier League
or new movies and video games.

You would have to swim through dark
freezing pressurised water luring
vile-tasting things with your light
and mating with an ugly fish if you
were really, really lucky. Even an ant
has a better life, at least knowing
sunlight and being able to see things
and not being a totally ugly bastard

warped by tons of pressure and cold
and lonely and bored all the time.
If you fell ill there would be no
hospitals or Get Well cards or fruit
just an agonising, lonely death
with your own relatives or worse
devouring your rotting remains
and crapping them out in the depths.

If those fish down there truly think
they are just as happy as us they are
totally deluded and in a state of
coping self-deception, the same way
poor people kid themselves they are
happier than rich people or dullards
think they are just as accomplished
as the educated and cultured.

Those ugly fish lacked the ambition
to improve themselves, settling
for a crappy existence while we
had the balls to seek out a better
life for ourselves on dry land with
coffee shops and touch-screens
and all the other totally entertaining
things that daily enrich our lives.

So never let me catch you whining
about your life when you could be
an ugly, unambitious fish swimming
around in freezing darkness with
a preposterous light on your head
without a Netflix subscription or any
qualifications and generally disliked
and unwanted, like a floating whale turd.

John D. Kelly

The Rainless Moon

Drought and famine reigned
for over two years from 1967.

Over 1.5 million humans died
of hunger and thirst.

I remember it well.
The First World looked on,

momentarily, then averted eyes
from Biafra, towards the stars

in outer space and to the fiery
priapic missiles of the cold-

hearted, Cold War boy-racers;
while flies, on black and white

T.V.'s, drank from the salty
tears in broken mothers' eyes.

*

In July 1969 an Eagle landed
on the rainless moon

at a cool, umbrella cost of over
25 billion dollars, at that time.

*

And today it seems like déja vu.
We have a new breed of wankers.

And I see food banks in a 'First'
World of new desperate mothers

flooded with new tears and pain
in this icy, dry reign of greed.

And they still build big, shiny
rocket-ships for the likes of

Captain James T. to go—coldly—
to where no man is, yet, hungry.

John Ling

Boiler suit

For the whole of his life
it was his uniform,
the spark burned boiler suit
that shielded him from the
angry blue white blaze
of the welding rod. Rode it
on his bike to work, wore it
at home at dinner time.
Last week's always hung
on the line in the yard,
so everyone knew this was
the home of a working man.

On Sundays it was trousers ,
rolled up sleeves for the
Allotment, non-working man,
his other face, his real,
patient man's face. But
going out in public, always,
the dark blue suit and tie.
Where we now dress down
he would dress up, shrugging
off the dirt, sweat and toil.

Now, my dungarees lie
folded in the wardrobe.
For me to wear them, would
need to be hard dirty work,
like he did every working
day of his entire life.

Gillian Mellor

Entitlement

The man with no mask doesn't move
behind the screen,
doesn't believe the science,

could slide his fingers inside
the gap between my mask and my face.
deems my eyes threatening *for a woman.*

> The last time we pressed the panic button
> HR phoned two days later and asked
> if there had been a knife at anyone's throat.
>
> No, but his goading sharpened our responses
> to the barrage of harassment over the phone.
> Of course there was panic. Our twisted faces
>
> sick with displays of pure fatigue.
> We remembered our subservient roles -
> there were other people in
>
> to watch the shitshow
> with prescriptions for anxiolytics of their own.
> It would've been different if he'd taken
>
> a bottle of scent without paying.
> But stealing the staff's safe space?
> That's hard to catch on CCTV.

What does a safe space smell like?
asked the woman from HR.
I didn't know, but its loss felt cold

on my skin. The hackles on my neck
stood up when the HR woman insisted
we refrain from panicking again.

The maskless man says he'll complain.
This will be over soon, I think.
Time yawns like a watched clock.

Another piece of me falls onto the carpet.
I retrieve it with my foot.
I do not let him see.

Jenny Mitchell

Levelling Up

They will not show this on the evening news—
our mother kneeling down at Number Ten—
a place of work and routine bacchanals—
to scrub red wine stains from the office carpet.
As vomit hits the wall above her head,
the PM wipes their chin, glass held in the air.

Spit flies out of their mouth, pollutes the air,
with yet another garbled toast to *A new
day*—just like the old, the PM standing at the head,
to help their chosen people keep control. Ten
men and women dance around the carpet,
close to mother's arm, to cheer the bacchanal.
The PM sees mum then, mouths *Bacchanal*,
shouting that *A cleaner's head is full of air!*
They explain the word, feet spread on the carpet,
followed by *You've missed a spot, old girl.* New
crates of wine are plonked onto the table, ten
bottles still with dregs, music coming to a head.

Our PM starts a waddling dance, nods their head,
wine spilling from the glass to toast the bacchanal
as they sing out of tune *The Winner Takes It All* ten
times, louder-still as Abba fades into the fetid air.
Mother tries to crawl away but catcalls are renewed
for her to polish shoes, kneeling on the carpet.

The PM joins in with this call, offers mum ten
pounds to lick the leather clean, then shouts *The carpet*
has to be made new, aims a kick at mother's head,
falling in a heap, demanding to be helped. The air
is filled with threat they won't show on the news,
even when we know about the many bacchanals.

Ten people and the PM drink their fill—a bacchanal
for the lawmakers, sore-headed the next day, air
rank with sick still on a carpet mother must renew.

Alan Morrison

The Shouting Tories

There's a sound that hounds the souls of the poor,
That rumbles louder than empty bellies:
Green benches of Tories shouting *"MORE!—MORE!"*

Mice of indigence drowned out by the roar
Of privileged lions shiver like jellies
To the sound that hounds the souls of the poor.

While pensioners shiver, frosted with hoar,
As energy giants put them into deep freeze
Green benches of Tories boom *"MORE!—MORE!"*

The ominous rustle & thump through the door
Of brown envelopes marked DWP,
Another sound that hounds the souls of the poor.

Fleeced private renters sponge-wiping mould spores
To churning coughs of black damp allergies,
As Tory slum landlords shout *"MORE!—MORE!"*

Louder than muzak in the monstrous thrift store,
Or the plastic tap of PIP assessors' keys,
There's a sound that hounds the souls of the poor:
Green benches of Tories shouting *"MORE!—MORE!"*

Liam O'Neill

Mr Cameron's Foodbank
(or, When Tone-Deaf Privilege Fails To Read the Room)

He hung out at the Guildhall
packing food for the hungry poor,
the Lord of Chipping Norton
passing alms, and a little humility,
to the assembled press.

Where was this altruism when he took a gutting knife to welfare nets?

Where was this humanity when he capped supports for the working poor?

Cameron, Osborne, Clegg
(Sounding like a team of legal receivers)
pledged to eradicate child poverty throughout the UK,
then set-out to asset-strip the last layers of economic
protection from the post-war social contract.

*Dare they take bread from the middle incomes, upon which, their voting
base depends?*

*Dare they take bread from the wealthy plutocrats, upon which, their party
coffers derive?*

It's always been the voiceless, of course,
and the powerless, of course,
and those without protections, of course,
whose larders get raided first.

And now he is here, before us,
the Lord of Chipping Norton;

a failed, old, amnesiac dispensing
compassion and necessities in some
perverse game of disavowment and abdication.
Greatly unaware in his tone-deaf,
privateering brain, that the seeds of the
next revolution are sown in the
food bank/soup-kitchens of the world.

Yes, the Lord of Chipping Norton
smiles wide for the waiting press
and the decent people impoverished
by the economic policies
he spearheaded into power.

And the poor, funnelled into this queue,
accept Cameron's donations
with polite British thanks;
their stomachs too hungry
to make a fuss,
and mouths too dry
to spit.

Ciarán O'Rourke

Concerning the Conditions of the Working Poor
After Friedrich Engels, 1820-1895

A two-hundred-thousand mass—and what a mass!
Bare women, ruddy men, with nothing left, completely
clad in rags: living proletarians,
and more—of Ireland, each and all, feral,
fierce, fanatic Gaels... give me
two hundred thousand of such stock
and we could overthrow the monarchy tomorrow!
Hunger drives them here, to ice-cold,
mechanised, fair England's halls:
in the brutal hurly-burly of the factories
their restiveness takes root: they squander
what they earn, then starve until
the next pay-day, on less and less, too much
accustomed (never reconciled)
to the pang between their ribs. All this
brings out the wayward contradictions
of the age, and in their nature: dissonant
and dumb, low-simmering in rage, they lash back
blindly at the great metropolis, the savageries
they bear, thirsting always for revenge—
these poorest of the poor, slum-
wracked and huddled with the dregs.
At home, meanwhile, among
the waste, abandoned fields, the ruins
grow like weeds: medieval churches,
ancient megaliths, and farther west,
the stony huts of peasants, rotting in the rain,
famine shaking like a palsy
across the stunted hills. Beyond

these shrunken villages, long avenues of loss,
a splendid greenery survives—on lawns
the leisured landlords keep in fine repair.
We find, in this, a demonic iteration
of imperial excess! But the rising,
beggared people see it plain: a plunder-
loving caste and nation, built
on human dispossession, forging its own chains.

Antony Owen

Our Street Of Ghosts

I remember when Thatcher killed all our fathers
we gazed at snow making alps of factory rooftops
an orange Cortina billowed in the distance
"Men who make great cars drive shit ones" Dad said.

My Dad's took up vaping for the hell of it
I think he misses the thrill of the real thing
smoking inside his ark afloat on a tulip sea
building his ovum of old Cortina parts.

My Dad sees Nineteen Eighty in Twenty Twenty-Two
he said *"Maggie and Boris killed a part of me in you"*
My Father's hair now resembles that snowy factory roof
it covers the stained-glass of his derelict eyes.

Last night he vacced my fake grass free of real leaves
a bee pulsed on the wilting lavender
it had lost the will to return to its hive
the death of summer is odourless.

I don't work with people anymore just for them
we talk on zoom and sometimes a dog barks
or a baby face bombs the meetings
you get a warning for that now.

I keep having this dream where my mask won't come off
and my dad is trapped in a machine but stays there,
he is producing a malfunction and laughter.
I think he wants to meet his maker.

Ian Parks

Marston Moor

I've come to the edge of the arable land
where the straight swords are crossing on the map
in a time of indecision and a time of change.
There, on the far side of the swale,

a wall of pikes held back the Royalist horse
and where the thin hedge peters out
men from the same country shot them down.
Some say it's for the best the houses come

to sink their deep foundations in the soil.
For now they're out of sight and out of range.
So let the dead lie undisturbed
where every rise and dip in that bare ground

marks out the places where they fell
and come here when the sun is sinking low
over the scrub, the footpaths, and the plain
in a time of indecision and a time of change.

Tracey Pearson

Somewhere a Tory Flaps its Wings

a foodbank volunteer   pretends not to know
her neighbour   adds an extra packet of biscuits

a child eats cereal for breakfast   dinner
and tea   now poverty's on the menu

a veteran sleeps in a tent   under a bridge
waits for the day   the bombs stop

a mental health support worker   pops
an antidepressant   prays for a quiet day

a young man   drives his van   through
every page of the A-Z   making Amazon drops

a widow   remembers her wedding day
as she fills in the Bereavement Support form

a striker raises a banner   explains again
about fair pay   job cuts   security   rights for all

a single mother   goes to the Job Centre   knowing
the job she wants   doesn't want the likes of her

an old man kisses his pint   leans into
the bar for comfort   misses his shipyard

an interviewer asks the Westminster liar   if he cares
he ruffles his hair   smirks   answers a different question

somewhere   Love flaps its wings   the tired people
begin to believe   rise up   and sing

Steve Pottinger

(don't) read all about it!

In all the stories from the funeral there's one that they don't tell:
it's how Kwasi's clearly off his chops or seriously unwell,
but the media stay silent, they decide this isn't news
instead they focus our attention on the pronouns people choose.
They laud a queue to see a coffin, ignore the ones for A&E,
print photographs of foodbanks with Conservative MPs
who are smiling for the camera, and never ask them how it is
that folk can work yet not afford to eat in this wealthiest of countries.
And if we start to grumble about what lies out of our reach
they're quick to point their lying finger at some poor sod on a beach
who's just landed in a dinghy, say that they're the ones to blame.
They set the poor upon the poorer, the same old sorry game
they've played down all the centuries, one that offers no solution,
which provides us with a scapegoat when we need some kind of revolution.
And yes, we're desperate and angry, and we sometimes take the bait
they're dangling in front of us. The politics of hate
can be attractive when you're powerless, when hope's in short supply,
when costs go up and wages don't. When rent's sky-high.
When the day-to-day is dismal and the future is a threat
and you could do with some distraction. And so, the trap is set
with flags and pageantry and outrage, they launch their war on woke™
and we're conscripted in a culture war against our own folk
where we're at each other's throats and all of us lose,
fighting on battlegrounds we didn't choose.
We need to do so much better than this. Bring ourselves back from the brink.
The world we want to live in is closer than we think
if we just look out for each other. Don't buy the lies they sell.
The stories that we need to hear are the ones that they don't tell.

Emma Purshouse

Unsuitable Places—the YTS girl from the Old Vic Hotel remembers

I hadn't thought of it for years. How the top floor
where they housed students from the polytechnic
was an obstacle course of leaky roof drips and drops

into pans. How the ballroom smelled of floor polish,
how the only things that ever danced there then
were dust motes. Hadn't thought of Pretty Mandy,

or Pretty Punky Mandy, or sweet Paulette's cow eyes
how they glamourised reception which was both booth,
shop window, and exhibit where punters would come

to check in, oggle and goggle at the charming
of switchboard snakes, deft handling of the SWEDA machine,
smoothing of pencil skirts, to make eye contact

in the slow palming of a key, ask about room service.
Hadn't thought of the duty managers, the blonde one
with the shadowy girlfriend, the dark one with the wandering hands

that were once tamed with the sharp edge of a ruler.
Hadn't thought of the yellowing chef with the fag hanging
at the corner of his mouth. The dropped rashers

slipped back into the pan, or the big black women
shuffling wordlessly under the weight of wrapped linen.
Hadn't thought about the mysterious night shifts

of live sex shows, coppers letting their hair down,
or the drinking in of squalid tales over shift change cuppas,
of being grossed out and not grossed out, shocked

and yet not shocked. Hadn't thought of it at all
til today. *Where is the humanity? the headline runs*
200 asylum seekers 'dumped' in city centre hotel.

Kid's faces pixilate in cracked frames. Hung out to dry
washing is bunting in first floor windows. A red jumper reaches
out its arms. Floral trousers press themselves to the glass.

Steve Taylor

The Red Wall

My parents didn't work hard enough
To become millionaires or send me to a private school.

They failed to own a grand estate or borrow
Against capital to invest. Their savings were paltry
Compared to bankers. Insubstantial. They employed
No staff or servants. No gamekeeper. Dad did
The privet hedge himself. There was no study
Or shelving stacked with books. We had no stables.

No tutor to teach me Greek.

I had to get my reading matter from the library
On Union Street next to the municipal swimming
Baths and the public laundry. We had a Gran

But she never owned land in Tsarist Russia. Or
Diamonds the size of potatoes to sell and see us right.

She had never known the gratitude of serfs.

I was never ashamed of my family
But they lacked the wherewithal to conquer Africa.

Neither Grandfather had the gumption to own a mine
Or mill. Both their wives had died in childbirth (but
I can't be blamed for that). Cancer killed the menfolk.

None of us rode to hounds or blasted grouse. We
Played no golf beyond the putting greens at Blackpool
Or Skegness. The crazy type in Scarborough.

When the Germans posed a threat we did our best
But never rose to Brigadier. You have to have ambition
To do that, to become someone better than you are. We
Weren't the worst of the poor but we sat amongst them.

I have inherited the laziness of my class I'm afraid.

Punish me.

Simon Tindale

working class blues

buying phoney lions
for their gated homes

under the illusion
they're joining the elite

affording them the privilege
to slag off their own

and all the public services
apart from the church

where they hedge their bets

someone should tell them
to go back
to where they came from

Rob Walton

The Magic of Other Bruces
(*In 1985 Bruce Springsteen donated $20,000 to miners' support groups*)

Bruce Straughan is a dab hand at trumpet cleaning.
You should see him handle lacquer cloth,
silver cloth, lint-free cloth and oil.
A few minutes with his valve-casing brush,
and Hey Presto! Perfect sounds!
What Mr. S doesn't know about mouthpiece brushes and sterilising spray
could be written on the back of a very small Big Meeting badge.

Bruce Haswell can turn his hand to sorting banners
when the silk is wearing thin.
He'll help with fetching and carrying beforehand—
Izzy Whizzy, Bruce gets busy—
and lends a hand if you're unsteady
on your pins on the cobbles on the march.
He does some sort of sleight of hand when he packs a holdall
with cans and crisps and sandwiches.
Abracadabra! A bar in a bag!

Then there's Bruce Kornett who's good at remembering
and reminding us to learn from the past
and telling us however bad things are
there's always hope in the green fields
at the end of the road.
He warns of the dangers of scapegoats
and teaches kinder ways.
He points out love and trust and says we should
hold banners in blue skies and grey
in sunshine and rain.

Bruce tells us the march goes on
and the magic of the Big Meeting must go on
to honour the past and fight for the future.

The party's only just begun
we'll have paper plates
made from papier-mâché
made from red gas bills

we'll have pass the parcel
passing two pence pieces
wrapped in our neighbours' wills

we'll have pin the tail
on the wonky donkey
that looks good enough to eat

we'll have charades
sitting on the floor
in the absence of a three-piece suite

we'll have jelly
and something like ice cream
and seriously diluted squash

we'll have crisps
and triangular sandwiches
and a game called under the cosh

we'll say so long
and give the guests
a useful sort of a prize

we'll hand out plastic-free party bags
with manifestos
and a call to rise

The Bruces say we should smile and laugh sometimes
and get angry and protest at other times.

Let's hear it for the Bruces.

David Williams

Closed

I wasn't sure whether I could put the word 'arseholes' in a poem
So, I thought I'd best leave it out, cos I don't want an old trout with gout
to shout "Language!"
It's a load of old tripe is or are onions.
"You won't get jellied eels or pie and mash around here now me old china"
cos everywhere has closed down.
Spice is putting the high in main street because everybody is down.
I remember Rhyl in 1983.
I'd just passed my driving test and there was a singer in the high street
Warbling songs from the Second World War,
his black T shirt clinging to his belly.
They called it a recession but it was pure depression.
I pulled into a lay-by on my way home and I cried.
I was 17 and the whole place had died.
Those boarded up shops, back then, are with us still
Peeling posters and stickers behind a red and black grill
The shutters on shops are the styes in our eyes.
If you can't buy nothing, you can't eat pies.
It's the same shade of government now as was back then
The people are so divided they'll never say 'When'
Enough is never enough for those at the top
They'll bleed us dry and they will not stop.
Profit and expansion are the name of the game
They want the poor at the bottom to all think the same.
They've divided and conquered us so much we don't know who to blame.
I'll end this poem in the same way as the start
And shout 'Arseholes' because everywhere's closed.

Joe Williams

Jacob Marley's Ghost Returns to London

I saved you, Ebenezer,
but I could have done much more.
We were not the only ones
blinded by venality.
This city is the proof of it,
these spires of Mammon,
built on all the sin I sought
to turn you away from,
though it was too late for me.

We lived in times of change,
you and I, Ebenezer.
Those who saw what we could not
made sure of that, yet still,
there are people going hungry
in this wealthiest of cities,
replete with fruits and spices
we could never dream of tasting,
flush with the plunder of the world.

I believed all the rich men
would fall, Ebenezer,
but no—they have more now
than we could have imagined.
I should not have undervalued
the resilience of greed,
the resolve of men with power
to absolve themselves of guilt,
transfer the stench of blame to the oppressed.

What say you, Ebenezer—
will you join me tonight?
There is a great deal of work to be done.